Learning Short-take®

CREATIVE BUSINESS THINKING

Developing the skills for thinking outside the box

CATHERINE MATTISKE

TPC - The Performance Company Pty Ltd
Level 20, Darling Park
Tower 2, 201 Sussex Street,
Sydney NSW 2000
Australia

ACN 077 455 273
email: tpc@tpc.net.au
Website: www.catherinemattiske.com

© TPC – The Performance Company Pty Limited
First edition published in 2006
Second edition published in 2011
Third edition published in 2022

All rights reserved. Apart from any fair dealing for the purposes of study, research or review, as permitted under Australian copyright law, no part of this publication may be reproduced by any means without the written permission of the copyright owner. Every effort has been made to obtain permission relating to information reproduced in this publication.

The information in this publication is based on the current state of commercial and industry practice, applicable legislation, general law and the general circumstances as at the date of publication. No person shall rely on any of the contents of this publication and the publisher and the author expressly exclude all liability for direct and indirect loss suffered by any person resulting in any way from the use of or reliance on this publication or any part of it. Any options and advice are offered solely in pursuance of the author's and the publisher's intention to provide information, and have not been specifically sought.

For eBook version: By payment of the required fees, you have been granted the non-exclusive, non-transferable right to access and read the text of this e-book on screen. No part of this text may be reproduced, transmitted, downloaded, decompiled, reverse engineered, or stored in or introduced into any information storage retrieval system, in any form or by any means, whether the electronic or mechanical, now known or hereinafter invented, without the express permission of the author.

 A catalogue record for this book is available from the National Library of Australia

National Library of Australia
Cataloguing-in-Publication data

Mattiske, Catherine
Creative Business Thinking: Developing the Skills for Thinking Outside the Box

ISBN 978-1-921547-25-6

1. Occupational training 2. Learning I. Title

370.113

Distributed by TPC - The Performance Company - www.catherinemattiske.com
For further information contact TPC - The Performance Company, Sydney Australia on +61 (02) 9555 1953.

HELLO.

Welcome to the Learning Short-take® process!

This Learning Short-take® is a bite sized learning package that aims to improve your skills and provide you with an opportunity for personal and professional development to achieve success in your role.

This Learning Short-take® combines self study with workplace activities in a unique learning system to keep you motivated and energized.
So let's get started!

Step 1:
What's inside?

- Learning Short-take®. This section contains all of the learning content and will guide you through the learning process.
- Learning Activities. You will be prompted to complete these as you read through.
- Learning Journal. This is a summary of your key learnings.
  Update it when prompted.
- Skill Development Action Plan. Learning is about taking action. This is your action plan where you'll plan how you will implement your learning.

Step 2:
Complete the Learning Short-take®

- Learning Short-takes® are best completed in a quiet environment that is free of distractions.
- Schedule time in your calendar to complete the Learning Short-take® and prioritize this time as an investment in your own professional development.
- Depending on the title, most participants complete the Learning Short-take® from 90 minutes to 2.5 hours.

Step 3:
Meet with your Manager/Coach

- Schedule a 30 minute meeting with your Manager or Coach.
- At this meeting share your completed Activities, Learning Journal and Skill Development Action Plan.
- Most importantly, discuss and agree on how you will implement your learning in your role.

GET VIP ACCESS TO YOUR MATERIALS

This Learning Short-take® includes an interactive activity book, associated tools and job aids, plus a bonus eBook.

1 Visit
https://www.catherinemattiske.com/books

2 Select your book

3 Click: 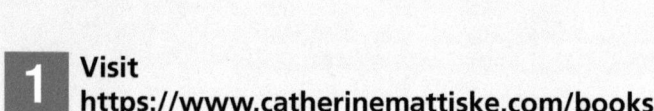 VIP ACCESS

4 Enter the code: CBT2022108

WELCOME

Creative Business Thinking
Developing the Skills for Thinking Outside the Box

Creative Business Thinking includes a library of brilliant creativity tools, fun activities, and challenging business scenarios. These will help to stretch your thinking by deliberately challenging existing perspectives and considering alternative ways of working.

Creative Business Thinking is packed with techniques for creative thinking and fun "mind quiz" activities. **Creative Business Thinking** constructively challenges the status quo to enable new ideas to surface and solve problems in ways that may not initially come to mind.

Within each of us there exists an infinite capacity for creating ideas and nurturing them through to innovation. **Creative Business Thinking** emphasizes pragmatic tools and techniques to successfully unlock creative potential.

Creative Business Thinking includes the job aid **15 Creativity Techniques for Problem Solving**, and the **Creative Business Thinking Techniques Wall Chart**, provided to you as free downloadable tools.

Now let's get started!

1	Learning Short-take® >	Start here
2	Learning Journal	77
3	Skill Development Action Plan	83
4	Quick Reference	89
5	Next Steps	111

"The answer to your problem 'pre-exists'. You need to ask the right question to reveal the answer."

CHARLES CHIC THOMPSON

"*Creative thinking is not a talent,
it is a skill that can be learnt.
It empowers people by adding
strength to their natural abilities which
improves teamwork, productivity and
where appropriate profits.*"

EDWARD DE BONO

Section 1
LEARNING SHORT-TAKE®

WHAT'S IN THIS LEARNING SHORT-TAKE®

"Imagination is the living power and prime agent of all human perception."

SAMUEL TAYLOR COLERIDGE

Table of Contents

How to Complete Your Learning Short-take®	5
Activity Checklist	6
Learning Objectives	7
Let's Get Started	8
Part 1 - Creativity Defined	9
Part 2 - Unleash those Creative Forces	21
Part 3 - Personal Creative Thinking Techniques	29
Part 4 - Creative Business Thinking for Groups	39
Part 5 - Answers	71

HOW TO COMPLETE YOUR LEARNING SHORT-TAKE®

1. Follow this Learning Short-take® by actively reading each section and highlighting key points as you go.

2. When directed, stop and complete activities.

3. When directed or at any time, stop and update your Learning Journal (located with your activities).

4. On completion (when you have finished all activities, updated your Learning Journal and created your Skill Development Action Plan) meet with your Manager/Coach to review your progress and establish an action plan.

5. Subject to your coach's final review and assessment, you will either sign off the Learning Short-take® as complete, or undertake further skill development as appropriate.

"Anyone can be creative provided they learn and develop their skills."

EDWARD DEBONO

ACTIVITY CHECKLIST

During this Learning Short-take® you will be prompted to complete the following activities:

- Activity 1 - Creativity Self Assessment — 18
- Activity 2 - Your Organization and Its Creativity — 27
- Activity 3 - Enhancing Personal Creativity — 37
- Activity 4 - Brainstorming & Variations — 49
- Activity 5 - Making Metaphors — 54
- Activity 6 - Mind mapping or SCAMMPERR — 61
- Activity 7 - Six Thinking Hats — 68
- Activity 8 - Planning your Next Meeting — 70
- Learning Journal — 77
- Skill Development Action Plan — 83

"No idea is so outlandish that it should not be considered with a searching but at the same time steady eye."

WINSTON CHURCHILL

LEARNING OBJECTIVES

By the end of this Learning Short-take® you should be able to:

- Undertake a self assessment in creativity
- List personal and organizational creative contributions
- Choose personal creative techniques to be used in the workplace
- Match group creativity techniques with case study applications
- Use six thinking hats to solve a business challenge
- Create a plan for an upcoming team meeting employing creative thinking techniques.

"A truly creative person rids him or herself of all self-imposed limitations."

GERALD G. JAMPOLSKY

LET'S GET STARTED

"Ideas are the root of creation.."

ERNEST DIMNET

In the business world today, creativity is in high demand. We are continually challenged to contribute new and fresh ideas in order to compete, survive and prosper.

Organizations seek ongoing innovation, encouraging employees to develop original ideas and concepts, and converting these into new products and services.

Creativity is the process of generating something new that has value. Before we can have innovation, we must have creativity. Some people excel when they are required to be creative. They seem to be born innovators. Regardless of whether you are highly creative naturally, or not, you can develop your creative business thinking skills.

This Learning Short-take® will allow you to practice creative thinking, put it into practice, and provide tools to use which should lead you to be more skilled at thinking creatively, alone or in a group.

CREATIVITY DEFINED

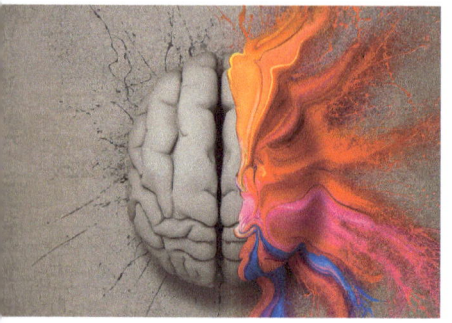

What is Creativity?

Creativity is bringing an item, a method or an idea which did not previously exist into reality. Creativity can be used to make existing products, processes and services better. It is expected that increasing your creativity will not only help you, but also your corporation and customers through improvements to a product or service.

Mind-Quiz # 1

Connect the dots by drawing four straight, continuous lines, and never lifting the pencil from the paper.

What is Creative Thinking?

Creative thinking is the process in which we construct a new idea. It is the merging of ideas which have not been put together before.

Techniques for Creative Thinking

There are a number of powerful techniques that can be used to develop new ideas and spark creativity. These techniques compel us to merge a wide range of ideas to generate new thoughts and processes. Techniques, such as brainstorming, are widely used to create an environment conducive to creative thinking.

Random acts of creativity!

Occasionally, we stumble upon an idea or an improvement unconsciously. Although this may not be intentional, it can still be considered creative thinking and is often referred to as 'accidental creative thinking'.

What is Lateral Thinking?

Lateral Thinking™ is a more systematic approach to creativity by deliberately using specific steps and techniques to think creatively. Instead of relying solely on logic, lateral thinking is a deliberate, systematic process to think differently.

Lateral thinking systematically forces thinking towards insight, creativity and innovation.

Techniques that apply lateral thinking to problems are characterized by the shifting of thinking patterns away from entrenched or predictable thinking to new or unexpected ideas.

A new idea that is the result of lateral thinking is not always a helpful one, but when a good idea is discovered it is usually obvious in hindsight, which is a feature lateral thinking shares with a joke.

Lateral Thinking is a term coined by Edward de Bono, a Maltese psychologist, physician, and writer. De Bono defines Lateral Thinking as methods of thinking concerned with changing concepts and perception. Lateral thinking is about reasoning that is not immediately obvious and about ideas that may not be obtainable by using only traditional step-by-step logic.

Benefits of Lateral Thinking

- Constructively challenge the status quo to enable new ideas to surface.
- Find and build on the concept behind an idea to create more ideas.
- Solve problems in ways that don't initially come to mind.
- Use alternatives to liberate and harness the creative energy of the organization.
- Turn problems into opportunities.
- Select the best alternate ideas and implement them.

Mind-Quiz # 2

It took two hours for two men to dig a hole five feet deep. How deep would it have been if 10 men had dug the hole for two hours?

Are you sure that's the only answer?

Check your answer on page 72

Thinking outside the box

"Thinking outside the box" is a cliché used to refer to looking at a problem from a new perspective without preconceptions, sometimes called a process of lateral thought. The catchphrase has become widely used in business environments, especially by management consultants, and has spawned a number of advertising slogans.

The Challenge

Connect the dots by drawing four straight, continuous lines, and never lifting the pencil from the paper.

One of many solutions:

The puzzle is easily solved, but only if you draw the lines outside of the confines of the square area defined by the nine dots themselves. Thus, the phrase "thinking outside the box" was born. Prof. Daniel Kies of the College of DuPage, observes that the puzzle is only difficult because "we imagine a boundary around the edge of the dot array".

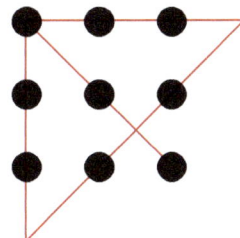

Christopher Columbus's Egg Puzzle as it appeared in Sam Loyd's Cyclopedia of Puzzles.

History

The nine dots puzzle is much older than the slogan. It appears in Sam Loyd's 1914 Cyclopedia of Puzzles.

In the 1951 compilation The Puzzle-Mine: Puzzles Collected from the Works of the Late Henry Ernest Dudeney, the puzzle is attributed to Dudeney himself.

Sam Loyd's original formulation of the puzzle called it "Christopher Columbus's egg puzzle."

Envisioning the target dots of the puzzle as eggs makes it clear that they have area and are not infinitesimally small points, or that the strokes that connect them have width.

Either of these features allows a three-line solution (near-parallel lines that meet far away from the nine points) or even a one-line solution (using a line thick enough to touch all nine points).

Critical Thinking coming in second!

Critical thinking involves logical thinking and reasoning skills such as comparison, classification, sequencing, cause/effect, patterning, webbing, analogies, deductive and inductive reasoning, forecasting, planning, hypothesizing, and critiquing.

Critical thinking tends to kill creative thinking.

For example, if you are brainstorming ideas and someone in the team starts criticizing ideas - even mildly - the creative process comes to a screeching halt. Given that no one wants their ideas criticized by the group - everyone begins to analyze their ideas before sharing. This results in watered down thinking and ideas.

Compare Critical Thinking to these Functions of Creative Thinking

Creative thinking involves creating something new or original.

It involves the skills of flexibility, originality, fluency, elaboration, brainstorming, modification, imagery, associative thinking, attribute listing, metaphorical thinking, and forced relationships.

The aim of creative thinking is to stimulate curiosity and promote divergence.

"Creativity, it has been said, consists largely of re-arranging what we know in order to find out what we do not know."

GEORGE KNELLER

In a business environment, critical thinking is usually about reducing risk.

Unfortunately, reducing risk almost always reduces creativity. The creative process is inevitably destroyed by the critical thinking process, with the best ideas sidelined following risk assessment and review. The result is a remarkably inefficient approach for generating mediocre ideas!

Therefore, we need to refine our use of critical thinking if we want to promote creativity. **It is far more effective to turn criticisms into challenges.** Instead of saying: "we don't have the budget for that!", say: "Interesting idea, but it would be difficult to get the budget to go ahead with it. In what ways might we reduce the cost of implementing your idea?" Instead of saying "Top management would never approve that!", say: "That's a great idea, but I am worried management will find it too radical. How might we sell the idea to them?".

Creativity vs. Innovation

Creativity is the process of generating new ideas. Any idea, even slightly different from something that already exists, is a creative idea.

Creativity is often confused with innovation, which is more about planning and implementing ideas. You can have 100 new ideas each day, but you are only innovative when you have successfully implemented one of them.

Thought Provoker

Creativity is seeing what everyone else sees and thinking something different.

So how do you think in different ways?

Mind-Quiz # 3

Complete Activity # 1
Creativity Self Assessment

ACTIVITY 1: CREATIVITY SELF ASSESSMENT

Test 1. Word Hints to Creativity

Find a fourth word that is related to all three words listed below. For example, what word is related to these? cookies, sixteen, heart. The answer is "sweet". Cookies are sweet; sweet is part of the word "sweetheart" and part of the phrase "sweet sixteen."

surprise, line, birthday		base, snow, dance	
rat, blue, cottage		nap, rig, call	
golf, foot, country		house, weary, ape	
tiger, plate, news		painting, bowl, nail	
proof, sea, priest		maple, beet, loaf	
oak, show, plan		light, village, golf	
merry, out, up		cheese, courage, oven	
red, star, house			

Test 2. Pictures Test Your Creativity

Depending on your reaction, say whether you like or dislike each of the following drawings (L for like and D for dislike).

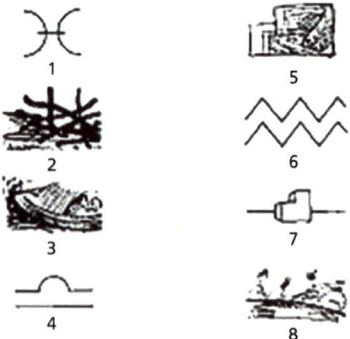

ACTIVITY 1: CONTINUED

Test 3. Which Traits Describe You?
Circle the adjectives that you believe really describe you.

determined	life-of-party	stern
responsible	dynamic	sociable
tolerant	polite	sensitive
independent	informal	restless
inventive	impulsive	reflective
enthusiastic	excitable	rational
clear-thinking	popular	preoccupied
understanding	cheerful	practical
individualistic	obedient	peaceable
industrious	self-demanding	organized
dependable	unassuming	moody
absent-minded	worrying	masculine
logical	polished	loyal
versatile	fashionable	good-natured

ACTIVITY 1: CONTINUED

Test 4. Random Questions
Answer A or B to each of the following questions:

				Answer A or B
1	Would you rather be considered:	A - A practical person?	B - An ingenious person?	
2	If you were a teacher, would you rather teach:	A - Fact courses?	B - Courses involving theory?	
3	Does following a schedule:	A - Appeal to you?	B - Cramp you?	
4	When there is a special job to be done, do you like to:	A - Organise it carefully before you start?	B - Find out what is necessary as you go along?	
5	Do you often get behind in your work?	A - yes	B - no	
6	Do you prefer specific instructions to those that leave many details optional?	A - yes	B - no	
7	Do hunches come to you just before going to sleep?	A - yes	B - no	
8	Do you often fret about daily chores?	A - yes	B - no	
9	Do you like to introduce the speaker at a meeting?	A - yes	B - no	
10	Do you get your best ideas when you are relaxed?	A - yes	B - no	
11	Do you sometimes feel anxious about the success of your efforts?	A - yes	B - no	
12	Do you like work in which you must influence others?	A - yes	B - no	
13	Are you fundamentally contented?	A - yes	B - no	
14	Do you like work that has regular hours?	A - yes	B - no	
15	Do you spend many evenings with friends?	A - yes	B - no	
16	As a child, were you inclined to take life seriously?	A - yes	B - no	
17	Do you frequently daydream?	A - yes	B - no	
18	Do you remember the names of people you meet?	A - yes	B - no	
19	Do you like to keep regular hours and run your life according to established routine?	A - yes	B - no	
20	Is it hard for you to sympathize with a person who is always doubting and unsure about things?	A - yes	B - no	

Now, Check your answers on pages 75 and 76.

Now update your Learning Journal (page 77)

UNLEASH THOSE CREATIVE FORCES

PART 2

UNLEASH THOSE CREATIVE FORCES

"Genius is one percent inspiration, and ninety-nine percent perspiration."

THOMAS EDISON

Individual creativity

Creativity is a natural skill that gets rusty when not used. Like playing a musical instrument, or a sport, some people seem naturally talented whilst others have to practice more to develop their skill. For many people there may be creative blocks to overcome.

Left-brain dominance has been long respected in organizations for its logic, reason and rationality. Creativity however requires the services of the right side of our brain that thinks outside the logical square. As a child we used our right brain to create dragons from cardboard boxes, and it is this type of thinking we need for challenges requiring creativity.

Three Limiting Beliefs

The primary blocks to our creative potential seem to originate from the limiting beliefs of a left-brain world:

- I am not creative
- It's not okay to be creative round here
- I don't know how to be creative

Ideas to overcome limiting beliefs

#1 - I'm not creative

A positive belief in your creative talent is essential. Recall how many times you have been creative, even in small ways. You may not have thought about creativity in this way before, but most people soon begin to realize how often they have been creative outside the work context.

As a child your imagination was at its peak. The innocent and free creative thinking you had as a child can be rekindled and put to use for your grown-up situations. As a small child you had very few opinions about the world.

Rigid opinions and quick judgments stifle creative thinking, so free your mind to have different thoughts and accept that there are many ways of perceiving a situation.

#2 - It's not okay to be creative here

Having learned to be creative you need the courage to do things differently. This may mean breaking rules and conventions, the barriers to creativity in your workplace.

It means being a leader and a role model, and encouraging others to be creative with you.

Stepping outside an organization's cultural norms can be a little scary, but there will be others who share the desire to be more creative and who may also be willing to share the risk.

With a balance of left and right brain thinking our workplaces can be more conducive to the generation of creative ideas.

"No problem is insurmountable. With a little courage, teamwork and determination a person can overcome anything."

B. DODGE

#3 - I don't know how

Developing creativity is the same as developing any skill. You have to learn about it and practice it regularly. Curiosity is a good place to begin. Samuel Johnson once said 'curiosity is one of the permanent and certain characteristics of a vigorous intellect'.

More than anything else, creativity is an attitude of mind which is developed through a curiosity to see things from different perspectives and to connect things from different contexts.

Think of two totally unconnected things and make a link between them, no matter how ridiculous the link may be. This is exactly what the inventor of cats' eyes in the road did - he made a connection between the cat and road safety. This is one of many techniques you can use to exercise your creative mind.

There is also an abundance of media, seminars, courses and consultants to help you develop creative thinking. This process of learning brings the changes you need for thinking and acting in ways that create new ideas and options for you and your organization.

Organizational creativity

Leading organizations are learning how to develop initiative and flexibility in their teams.

They are accepting mistakes as a route to good ideas and acknowledging the greater potential, which can be realized by having a supportive and sharing culture.

These beliefs connect people at a deep level in an organization and are the basic building blocks to developing a creative culture.

The key structural change they are making is in the development of flexible, multi-disciplinary teams where the output of creative ideas and productivity can be represented by the equation 1 + 1 = 3.

Developing a flexible team structure is often the most challenging stage in the pursuit of a creative culture that is embraced by employees as a way of life.

To achieve this people need to be engaged up-front in decision-making and fully involved in day-to-day improvements to operations.

Mind-Quiz # 4

ALTERNATIVE	ALTERNATIVE	ALTERNATIVE
ALTERNATIVE	ALTERNATIVE	ALTERNATIVE
ALTERNATIVE	ALTERNATIVE	ALTERNATIVE
ALTERNATIVE	ALTERNATIVE	ALTERNATIVE
ALTERNATIVE	**CHOICE**	ALTERNATIVE
ALTERNATIVE	ALTERNATIVE	ALTERNATIVE
ALTERNATIVE	ALTERNATIVE	ALTERNATIVE
ALTERNATIVE	ALTERNATIVE	ALTERNATIVE
ALTERNATIVE	ALTERNATIVE	ALTERNATIVE
ALTERNATIVE	ALTERNATIVE	ALTERNATIVE
ALTERNATIVE	ALTERNATIVE	ALTERNATIVE
ALTERNATIVE	ALTERNATIVE	ALTERNATIVE

What are organizations doing to harness creativity?

What are organizations doing to harness creativity? Organizations are embracing a wide range of options in their quest for creativity. There are simple and structured techniques like brainstorming and mind mapping commonly favored as creative tools for Quality programs.

Creative inspiration is also being drawn from many other contexts. The Walt Disney strategy for example is based upon the creative process Walt used to produce his most successful animated films and consists of three stages:

- **Dreamer** - the playful state of generating new ideas.
- **Realist** - putting reality into ideas and selecting the most appropriate.
- **Critic** - looking at details for ways to improve an idea.

Dreamers prefer to generate ideas while Realists prefer a more pragmatic approach to creativity. Critics enjoy checking the small details of others' ideas. Respecting these differences and bringing people together as multi-disciplinary teams makes a highly creative and effective team.

A leading news and financial information organization with thousands of staff worldwide, used a theme of 'working fast' in an effort to keep pace with technology and competition. They held running races in every corner of the globe at exactly the same time, challenging staff teams across the world to compete against each other. Employees were also rewarded when they presented creative ideas of how they could work faster as an entire organization.

Complete Activity # 2
Your Organization and Its Creativity

ACTIVITY 2: YOUR ORGANIZATION AND ITS CREATIVITY

How creative is your organization? Write a list of personal and organizational initiatives that you consider were 'creative' and made a valuable contribution to the organization.

Personal Creativity

When thinking of your personal contributions that you have made to the organization, think of both large projects that you've been involved with and also 'the little things' that you've developed (perhaps unnoticed) that have made a difference in efficiency, effectiveness or team morale.

What was the creative idea?	What was the impact?	Who was impacted?

Organizational Creativity

Organizations are creative with product development, customer service, how they bring a product to market and countless other forms of creativity. Also, organizations are creative with areas such as employee engagement, team morale, loyalty and talent selection. Think of ways your organization has shown its creativity. Perhaps your company intranet or internet site may spark some ideas.

What was the creative idea?	What was the impact?	Who was impacted?

Now update your Learning Journal (page 77)

"The world we have made as a result of the level of thinking we have done thus far creates problems we cannot solve at the same level of thinking at which we created them."

ALBERT EINSTEIN

PERSONAL CREATIVE THINKING TECHNIQUES

PART 3

PERSONAL CREATIVE THINKING TECHNIQUES

There are many things we can do to improve our creativity.
These include:

1. Create a creative atmosphere
2. Focus on a situation or goal
3. Maintain determination
4. Don't get it right, get it written.

1 - Create a creative atmosphere

All of our senses, what we see, hear, feel, taste, and touch influence our state of mind. A positive atmosphere contributes to a positive and creative state of mind.

Creating a creative place

Some people thrive in loud, people-filled areas with much activity. Others need quiet and calm to think clearly and creatively. Find that place, noisy or quiet, that makes you feel comfortable to free your mind allowing for creativity.

Find a place to walk

If you think best 'on your feet', find a hallway, sidewalk, or park where you can walk. Taking a break away from the office environment and walking either alone or with a colleague often sparks creativity.

Find a place to relax

If you do your best creative thinking in a relaxed environment, set up your office or a space at home with a good chair, paintings, lighting, music, fresh flowers, and anything else that will help you relax.

Use pictures for inspiration

Surround yourself with inspirational props. You might use magazines, digital image libraries, online searches, junk mail, lyrics to music or poetry to generate ideas.

2 - Focus on your situation or goal

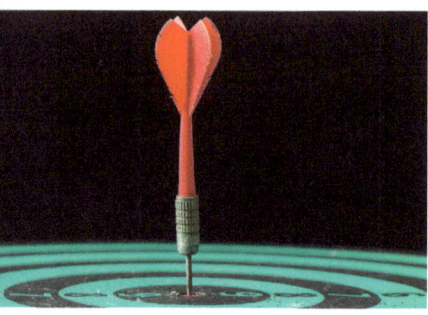

Without a specific goal in mind, random thoughts and ideas may not be particularly useful.

Define your problem, situation or goal

Take time to define what is happening - the 'as is' situation. Then, clearly identify your goal.

Similar situations

Take lessons from similar situations that you have faced in the past. What has worked well, and what could have worked better? By taking time to remember in detail a situation that has occurred before, allows the mind to build connections and ignite the thought process.

Metaphors for the situation

Search for parallels between familiarities in the situation you face. Often being outlandish can help spark creativity. For example: "organizing this event is like planning a military operation". Analyze the metaphor for similarities and write down connections. Often these connections will spark creative ideas.

Focus on your goals one by one

Treat each objective as the only goal. This frees you from trying to solve too many problems at the same time.

Reverse your goals

Generate ideas from thinking about what you want to avoid.

3 - Maintain Determination

Creativity takes practice

Your creativity is there within you, but you must make a habit of using your imagination. Although many of your best ideas will come when you "aren't really concentrating," you can make them happen more often by regularly practicing effective thinking techniques.

Schedule creative thinking

Even when not pondering a specific creative challenge, set aside a certain amount of time each day, week, or month to relax, brainstorm, and daydream. By getting in the habit of scheduling regularly creativity thinking time you'll be better able to meet future challenges as they arise.

Ponder on problems that don't exist

This isn't the same as worrying about things you can't change or trying to fix what isn't broken.

It means that even when you've come up with the perfect path to achieve your goals, think about alternatives.

Keep a file of ideas that were discarded as not feasible this time around. You may find inspiration for solving future problems and creative challenges.

Mind-Quiz # 6

4 - Don't get it right, get it written

Whether you use pen, pencil, crayon, or a computer, write down your ideas. We retain more of what we hear or see if we write it down.

Make notes any time, any place

Get in the habit of making notes, outlines, sketches, or doodles. If you are actively pursuing a specific idea or problem, always have paper and pencil or recorder at the ready. Jot down or record all your thoughts, no matter how "off-the-wall."

Keep a notebook by your bed

Some of your best thoughts come just before falling asleep and just after waking. Keep a notebook at your bedside so you will always be ready to write down ideas whenever they come.

Create an inspiration file

Whether it's a file folder, a notebook, an ideas board on your wall, a digital notes app or workspace, or an entire filing system, keep clippings, thumbnail sketches, junk mail, photos, useful links, digital images, videos or screenshots, and anything else that inspires you or gives you ideas.

Once created don't just file it and forget it. Go through the file during your scheduled creative thinking times and when actively pursing ideas for a project.

15 Creativity Techniques for Problem Solving

1. **Stop** thinking about the problem for a while and come back to it later.
2. **Think of other problems** that are similar to the one you're working on; either real or imaginary problems in real or imaginary domains. Solve those problems, and then translate the solution back to the original domain.
3. **Write down the problem**, and then translate it into various languages. Different languages divide things into concepts (words) in different ways, so this forces you to think about and recast the concepts that are involved.
4. **Explain the problem to someone.** For example, explaining a scientific problem to a layman, or to a scientist in a different field, forces one to think about the meanings of the concepts involved.
5. **State the problem differently**. Either in vague, broad terms or state it in much more specific, precise terms.
6. **Consume brain-enhancing nutrients** such as plenty of vitamin C, gingko extract, etc. Get some exercise, and have a snack just before your thinking session so you have adequate blood sugar levels.
7. **Think about the problem just before going to sleep.** Tell yourself you're going to dream about a solution to the problem. Put a pen and paper next to the bed so you can write down your dreams.
8. **Use your best time of day** ... morning, perhaps ... for creative thinking.

Mind-Quiz # 7

... EXCITEMENT EXCITEMENT EXCITEMENT EXCITEMENT EXCITEMENT EXCITEMENT EXCITEMENT EXCITEMENT EXCITEMENT EXCITEMENT EXCITEMENT EXCITEMENT EXCITEMENT EXCITEMENT EXCITEMENT EXCITEMENT EXCITEMENT EXCITEMENT...

9. **Visual images:** purposely think in visual images.
10. **Put pictures and objects around where you'll see them,** things that relate somehow to the problem.
11. **Change track earlier than a blockage.** For example, suppose you've been thinking over and over again, "A, therefore B, therefore C, therefore D, therefore E, and then where can I go from there?" There's a blockage at E: you haven't been able to progress from there. Well, take a different crossroad of thought earlier on. Rather than searching for a route from E, search for a different route from, say C, and follow it. "C, therefore X, therefore Y …"
12. **Imagine an alternate universe.** Assume something that's false, that will make the problem easier to solve. Solve the problem in that universe, and then see if the solution can be modified to work in this universe.
13. **Go into right brain mode.** Use music, rhythm, color, rhyme, abstraction to spark ideas.
14. **Broaden the perspective.** Ask why the problem exists at all, and redefine the problem as if to have this problem or challenge wasn't a problem at all!
15. **Record-keeping.** Keep a list of problems, recording how impossible they seem before they're solved. Looking back later on how many 'impossible-seeming' problems actually got solved can help fuel optimism about the search for solutions to new problems.

Download the summary job aid **15 Creativity Techniques for Problem Solving** from
https://www.catherinematttiske.com/books

Complete Activity # 3
Enhancing Personal Creativity

ACTIVITY 3: ENHANCING PERSONAL CREATIVITY

From the list below determine your professional development opportunities. Use your Learning Short-take® reference manual to prompt your memory of the detail of each creative technique.

For each technique, put a ✓ in one of the columns to the right.

	Mastered and use	Mastered but will now use more	Like the sound of it - will learn and use	Not for me!
1 - Create a creative atmosphere				
Creating a Creative Place				
Find a Place to Walk				
Find a Place to Relax				
Use Pictures for Inspiration				
2 - Focus on your situation or goal				
Define your problem, situation or goal				
Similar Situations				
Metaphors for the situation				
Focus on your goals one by one				
Reverse your goals				
3 - Maintain Determination				
Creativity takes practice				
Schedule Creative Thinking				
Ponder On Problems That Don't Exist				
4 – Don't get it right, get it written				
Make Notes Any Time, Any Place				
Keep a Notebook By Your Bed				
Create an Inspiration File				

Now, on the list above, highlight all techniques that you have checked as either 'Mastered, but will now use more' or 'Like the sound of it - will learn and use'.

Now update your Learning Journal (page 77)

© 2022, TPC - The Performance Company Pty Limited. All rights reserved.

"Creative novelty springs largely from the rearrangement of the existing knowledge, a rearrangement that is itself an addition to knowledge."

J. KNELLER

CREATIVE BUSINESS THINKING FOR GROUPS

PART 4

CREATIVE BUSINESS THINKING FOR GROUPS

Choosing appropriate methods

With so many options available it can be difficult to find the best methods for your organization or group. However, what is more important than the choice of method is the approach to working with groups. Here are some simple guidelines to help the manager or facilitator prepare the way for an enduring creative process:

- **Respect the group** - no one likes to be told they have been doing it all wrong, so show respect for past and current methods of idea creation. Help the group find the desire to be creative by asking questions about their future and the future of their markets, industry and customers.
- **Take your time, don't push too hard** - encourage the group to take ownership of the whole process.
- **Focus the group on its objectives** - if they don't have objectives, this is a good place to start.
- **Focus on the future** - don't dwell on current problems which are well known and which will serve to keep people fixed on habitual ways.
- **Link all activity and objectives clearly to business aims and results.**
- **Create environments that encourage natural creativity** - use music, activities, color, texture and space in creative ways.
- **If you use consultants, get references from their clients** - testimonials are vitally important for creative workshops or meetings.

Library of Creative Business Thinking Techniques

The following creative business thinking techniques have been provided for use in meetings, workshops and other facilitated sessions. Use the appropriate technique depending on the focus of the session.

Technique	Meeting focus			
	Idea Generation	Idea Implementation	Idea Selection	Problem / Situation Definition
Alternative Scenarios		✔		✔
Brainstorming	✔			
BrainWriting	✔			
Do Nothing	✔			
DO IT			✔	✔
Metaphors	✔			✔
Mind Mapping	✔			✔
Random Input	✔			
RoleStorming	✔			
SCAMMPERR	✔			
Six Thinking Hats	✔	✔	✔	

Alternative Scenarios
(Situation definition, Idea Implementation)

Scenarios can give you a deeper understanding of potential environments in which you might have to operate and what you may need to do in the present. Scenario analysis helps you to identify what environmental factors to monitor over time, so that when the environment shifts, you can recognize where it is shifting to.

Thinking through several scenarios is a less risky, more conservative approach to planning than relying on single forecasts and trend analyses. It can thus free up management to take more innovative actions.

Scenarios are developed specifically for a particular problem.
To begin developing scenarios:

- State the specific decision that needs to be made.
- Identify the major forces that impact the decision.
- Build four scenarios based on each of the major forces.
- Examine the links and synergies of opportunities across the range of scenarios. This would help you to formulate a more realistic business decision.

Brainstorming (Idea Generation)

Brainstorming has meeting attendees encouraged to think quickly and creatively: to generate creative ideas spontaneously, usually for problem-solving, and especially in an intensive group discussion that does not allow time for reflection.

Brainstorming is a creativity technique to generate ideas to solve a problem. The main result of a brainstorm session may be a complete solution to the problem, a list of ideas for an approach to a subsequent solution, or a list of ideas resulting in a plan to find a solution.

Brainstorming was originated in 1953 in a book called Applied Imagination by Alex F. Osborn, an advertising executive. Brainstorming has many applications but it is most often used in:

- New product development - obtaining ideas for new products and improving existing products.
- Advertising - developing ideas for advertising campaigns.
- Problem solving - issues, root causes, alternative solutions, impact analysis, evaluation.
- Process management - finding ways of improving business and production processes.
- Project Management - identifying client objectives, risks, deliverables, work packages, resources, roles and responsibilities, tasks and issues.
- Team building - generates sharing and discussion of ideas while stimulating participants to think.
- Business planning - develop and improve the product idea.

Facilitating a Brainstorming Session

- You will need a **large whiteboard** or **flipchart paper** on which to write and a large felt-tipped pen.
- **The question or issue is written up on the paper for all to see.**
- **Appoint a person as scribe.** The scribe must write down every idea as quickly as possible without censoring or qualification (abbreviation is allowed). The scribe may also act as the group motivator, constantly calling for new ideas. Alternatively, another person may take the motivator role. The scribe should work in front of the group. All ideas written up must be visible to the whole group.
- **Operate with a group of 7-10 people.** 15 people are generally the upper workable limit. Try to obtain a mix of people from different backgrounds, divisions, departments and disciplines.
- **Have the group define the task in clear terms.** Avoid self-limiting definitions. For example, instead of asking "How can we eliminate overtime?", as "How can we improve use of employee work hours?" The later question is more open and will give you more options.
- **Ask for crazy ideas early in the brainstorm session**. This will stimulate freewheeling ideas which go beyond the established wisdom and known solutions.

- **There should be no criticism or evaluation of ideas at this stage.** If someone disagrees with an idea, or doesn't think it feasible, they should not say so, but should offer an alternative idea (without explanation).
- **Seek a large number of ideas.** Their quality is irrelevant. Evaluation comes later.
- **Link different ideas together.** Expand on ideas. Play with them. Encourage the group to be lively - it is a catalyst of creativity.

- **Keep the pace fast.** Keep comments to a minimum. The scribe should stimulate the group: for example "That's great! Is there any other way we could do it?", "What else could we do?", "How else could it be done?"
- **Be aware of the group energy**. If the group has run out of ideas, move on to evaluation using the 80:20 rule, fish bone analysis, or any other useful process.
- **If the group is stuck and is beginning to evaluate brainstormed options ask: "What would you do if you had an unlimited budget and could spend a huge amount of money?"** Forcing participants to remove boundaries will most likely kick-start the discussion.

BrainWriting (Idea Generation)

BrainWriting is a technique similar to Brainstorming. There are many varieties, but the general process is that all ideas are recorded by the individual who thought of them. They are then passed on to the next person who uses them as a trigger for their own ideas. Examples of this include;

BrainWriting Pool

Each person, using Post-it notes or small cards, writes down ideas, and places them in the centre of the table. Everyone is free to pull out one or more of these ideas for inspiration. Team members can create new ideas, variations or piggyback on existing ideas.

Constrained BrainWriting

On a number of occasions you may want to constrain ideas around a pre-determined focus, rather than free wheeling. The versions described here use the standard BrainWriting pool technique, but bias the idea generation by using brain-writing sheets prepared in advance.

- **Present starter ideas:** The leader initiates the process by placing several prepared sheets of paper in the pool in the centre of the table (see note below).
- **Private BrainWriting:** Each group member takes a sheet, reads it, and silently adds his or her ideas.

- **Change sheet:** When a member runs out of ideas or wants to have the stimulation of another's ideas, s/he puts one list back in the centre of the table and takes one returned by another member. After reviewing this new list s/he has just selected, s/he adds more ideas.
- **Repeat until ideas are exhausted.** No discussion at any stage.

BrainWriting 6-3-5

The name BrainWriting 6-3-5 comes from the process of having 6 people write 3 ideas in 5 minutes. Each person has a blank 6-3-5 worksheet.

Problem Statement: How to...

	Idea 1	Idea 2	Idea 3
1			
2			
3			
4			
5			
6			

Everyone writes the problem statement at the top of their worksheet (word for word from an agreed problem definition). They then write 3 ideas on the top row of the worksheet in 5 minutes in a complete and concise sentence (6-10 words). At the end of 5 minutes (or when everyone has finished writing) pass the worksheet to the person on your right. You then add three more ideas. The process continues until the worksheet is completed.

There will now be a total of 108 ideas on the 6 worksheets. These can now be assessed.

Do Nothing (Idea Generation)

We often make the assumption that something must be done about a particular issue / problem, but what happens if we "do nothing"? Stop and think for a while, either alone or as a group, about the outcomes if nothing were done. This usually leads to one of three possible outcomes;

1. The problem doesn't need to be solved.
2. You will have a better idea of the benefits of solving the problem.
3. You will have generated some alternative problems to solve.

"The more you think, the more time you have."

HENRY FORD

Complete Activity # 4
Brainstorming & Variations

ACTIVITY 4: BRAINSTORMING & VARIATIONS

1. Using the Learning Short-take® as a guide, list ways you can improve your skills when facilitating a Brainstorming session.

2. What is the difference between Brainstorming and BrainWriting?

3. Define Constrained BrainWriting?

4. Identify an upcoming meeting, workshop or team gathering where you could use BrainWriting 6-3-5.

Now update your Learning Journal (page 77)

DO IT (Situation Definition & Idea Selection)

DO IT is an acronym that stands for:

- **D -** **D**efine problem or situation
- **O -** **O**pen mind and apply creative techniques
- **I -** **I**dentify best solution
- **T -** **T**ransform

Define Problem

Analyzing the problem to ensure that the correct question is being asked. The following points may help to do this:

- Check that you are tackling the problem, not the symptoms of the problem. To do this, ask yourself why the problem exists repeatedly until you get to the root of it.
- Lay out the bounds of the problem. Work out the objectives that you must achieve and the constraints that you are operating under.
- Where a problem appears to be very large, break it down into smaller parts. Keep on going until each part is achievable in its own right, or needs a precisely defined area of research to be carried out.
- Summarize the problem in as concise a form as possible.

Open Mind and Apply Creative Technique

Once you know the problem that you want to solve, you are ready to start generating possible solutions. It is very tempting just to accept the first good idea that you come across. If you do this, you will miss many even better solutions.

At this stage of DO IT we are not interested in evaluating ideas - we are trying to generate as many different ideas as possible. Even bad ideas may be the seeds of good ones.

Identify the Best Solution

Only at this stage do you select the best of the ideas you have generated. It may be that the best idea is obvious. Alternatively, it may be worth examining and developing a number of ideas in detail before you select one.

Transform

Having identified the problem and created a solution to it, the final stage is to implement this solution. This may take a great deal of time and energy.

Many very creative people fail at this stage. They will have fun creating new products and services that may be years ahead of what is available on the market. They will then fail to develop them, and watch someone else make a fortune out of the idea several years later!

"No matter how old you get, if you can keep the desire to be creative, you're keeping the man-child alive."

JOHN CASSAVETES

Metaphors
(Situation Definition, Idea Generation)

People knowingly and unknowingly use metaphors all the time. Many of these metaphors are expressions of our culture. They also give insight into the personal world views of people. Creatively used metaphors can help people look at a situation differently, opening up their frames of reference in a way that helps them see new possibilities.

> *In a previous meeting, our manager told us we'd failed to connect the dots on an important initiative. Consequently, what emerged was the metaphor of dots. It was very disconcerting and people were unenthusiastic about their work. Instead of taking a negative view of the dot metaphor our team decided to flip the concept into a positive one. In our next meeting, we were discussing how to work with key stakeholders across the organization in more productive ways. Our dot metaphor worked brilliantly. Each dot represented a different stakeholder. Creative thinking was required to connect the dots in ways that would create new perspectives for looking at a business challenges. The "connect-the-dots" metaphor was utilized as a vehicle to further our interpretation of what the possible solutions could look like. Using metaphors also led to new conceptualization. We referred to the "space" as the void of not getting together, created by our busy work lives which became a way of thinking about what was missing in our work when trying to influence, network and liaise with others in our organization.*

Ways to use metaphors:

- Call attention to metaphors when they are expressed and reflect on the implications, such as what they suggest about assumptions people are holding.

- Invite people to brainstorm metaphors for a particular situation with which a group is struggling.

- Use metaphors that speak from broad experiences common to the group, helping people become connected to the situation.

Complete Activity # 5
Making Metaphors

ACTIVITY 5: MAKING METAPHORS

Task 1 - Review Definition
The word 'Metaphor' comes from the Greek word metapherein - to transfer.
Metaphor is when we say X is Y such that Y is used to enhance the 'meaning' associated with X.

Task 2 - Write Definition in your own words
Using your own words, write a definition for Metaphor:

Task 3 - Metaphor Analysis:
1. Analyze the metaphors in column 1.
2. Determine what 'X' is – write it in Column 2.
3. Determine what 'Y' is – write it in Column 3.
4. Write the meaning of the metaphor in Column 4.

Metaphor	X	Y	Meaning
1. A steely gaze	*Gaze*	*Steely*	*Cold, hard and unyielding*
2. You can't make an omelette without breaking a few eggs			
3. Life is a dream			
4. Love is a mystery			
5. Silver is money			

ACTIVITY 5: CONTINUED

Metaphor	X	Y	Meaning
6. Gold is a sun			
7. Purple prose			
8. A land of milk and honey			
9. An ironclad attitude			
10. A hot temper			

Task 4 - Metaphors in your world

Reflect on situations and projects on which you are currently working. Create a metaphor for two projects or situations.

Project/Situation 1

Project Name / Situation

Metaphor

Project/Situation 2

Project Name / Situation

Metaphor

Now update your Learning Journal (page 77)

Why are those black dots jumping?

Is your perception, always reality?

"Begin challenging your own assumptions. Your assumptions are your windows on the world.

Scrub them off every once in a while, or the light won't come in."

ALAN ALDA

Mind Mapping
(Situation Definition or Idea Generation)

A mind map is a diagram used to represent words, ideas, tasks or other items linked to and arranged around a central key word or idea. It is used to generate, visualize, structure and classify ideas, and as an aid in concept development, problem solving, and decision making.

Mind mapping is an image-centered diagram that represents connections between portions of information. By presenting these connections in a radial, non-linear graphical manner, it encourages a brainstorming approach to any given organizational task, eliminating the hurdle of establishing an intrinsically appropriate or relevant conceptual framework to work within.

A mind map is similar to a semantic network or cognitive map but there are no formal restrictions on the kinds of links used. Most often the map involves images, words, and lines. The elements are arranged intuitively according to the importance of the concepts and organized into groupings, branches, or areas.

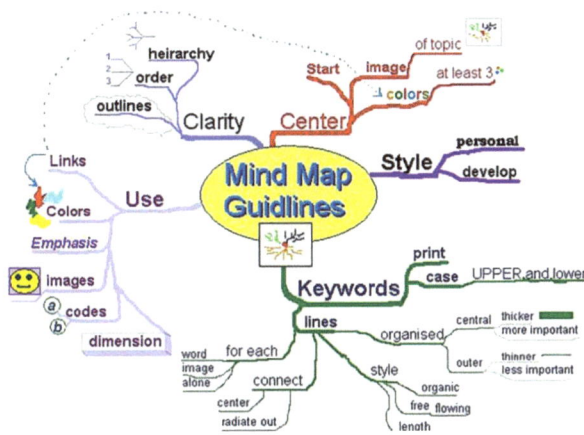

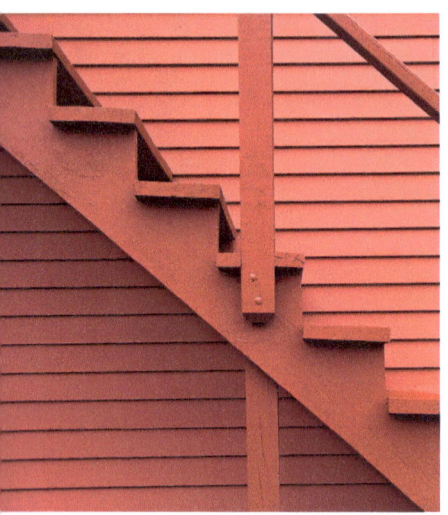

*"Creativity
is inventing,
experimenting,
growing, taking risks,
breaking rules,
making mistakes,
and having fun."*

MARY LOU COOK

Basic Mind Mapping Steps

- Start in the center with an image of the topic, using at least 3 colors.

- Use images, symbols, codes and dimensions throughout your mind map.

- Each key word/image must be alone and sitting on its own line.

- The lines must be connected, starting from the central image. The central lines are thicker, organic and flowing, becoming thinner as they radiate out from the center.

- Make the lines the same length as the word/image.

- Use colors - make up your own code - throughout the mind map.

- Develop your own personal style of mind mapping.

Random Input (Idea Generation)

Randomly pick up a magazine and read one article, no matter how remote its subject is to your challenge. Then contemplate the connections between the article and your challenge; try to generate some new ideas. Any such exercise is extremely valuable in helping you set up and cultivate habits that encourage random input.

RoleStorming (Idea Generation)

RoleStorming is an evolution of Brainstorming, whereby you take on another identity. Viewing problems and solutions from a different standpoint. Unusual 'off the wall' ideas may seem radical/'silly' if 'you' present them, however, generated by a nameless person removes any embarrassment.

Use traditional brainstorming or other idea generating technique as a start point

- Invent an identity or use that of someone you know.
- Assume that identity or refer to the fictitious person as 'this person would suggest…..'
- Brainstorm (or use other idea-generating techniques) in separate identity.
- Change roles. Now try another identity obviously this can be done many times for many different characters.

SCAMMPERR (Idea Generation)

SCAMMPERR is a check list that helps you to think of changes you can make to an existing product or service to create a new one. You can use these changes either as direct suggestions or as starting points for lateral thinking.

The changes SCAMMPERR stands for are:

S -   Substitute - components, materials, people
C -   Combine - mix, combine with other assemblies or services, integrate
A -   Adapt - alter, change function, use part of another element
M -   Magnify - Make it enormous, longer, higher, overstated, added features
M -   Modify - increase or reduce in scale, change shape, modify attributes (e.g. color)
P -   Put to another use
E -   Eliminate - remove elements, simplify, reduce to core functionality
R -   Rearrange - change the order, interchange components, change the speed or other pattern
R -   Reverse - turn inside out or upside down

Complete Activity # 6
Mind mapping or SCAMMPERR

ACTIVITY 6: MIND MAPPING OR SCAMMPERR

You choice! Review the sections of the Learning Short-take® for Mind Mapping and SCAMMPERR. Choose one skill to develop.

Circle one: I have chosen: Mind Mapping   SCAMMPERR

Complete your chosen task below:

Mind Mapping

Task 1 - Practice Mind Mapping. Your task list.

Create a mind map of your current tasks and projects.

1. Get a blank sheet of paper, and turn it to landscape / sideways.
2. In the center of the page, begin your mind map by drawing a circle or cloud shape. In bold letters write: "My tasks as at [date]".
3. Then, using major branches from the center, put your major themes. For example, administration, client work, team communication, projects and so on. Use words that have most meaning for you.
4. Break down each branch into individual projects.
5. Continue to add detail to each branch until you get to outstanding tasks for each project.
6. Add symbols, icons and color to highlight key areas of your mind map.
7. [Feel free to jump around your mind map working on different branches as ideas spring to mind].

Task 2 - Application of Mind Mapping

1. Where can you use the technique of mind mapping?

2. How will you use it?

3. Who else could you teach mind mapping to? What would be the benefit to them?

ACTIVITY 6: CONTINUED

SCAMMPERR

Task 1 - Practice SCAMMPERR. An existing product - a refrigerator!

Take a moment to think about the refrigerator in your kitchen. In your minds eye focus on what it looks like on the outside and the inside. What features does it have? If you had to sell this refrigerator, what are its selling points? Now, let's imagine a better refrigerator.

Complete the following SCAMMPERR and see what you can create!

S	Substitute	components, materials, people	
C	Combine	mix, combine with other assemblies or services, integrate	
A	Adapt	alter, change function, use part of another element	
M	Magnify	Make it enormous, longer, higher, overstated, added features	
M	Modify	increase or reduce in scale, change shape, modify attributes (e.g. color)	
P	Put to another use		
E	Eliminate	remove elements, simplify, reduce to core functionality	
R	Rearrange	change the order, interchange components, change the speed or other pattern	
R	Reverse	turn inside out or upside down	

Task 2 - Application of SCAMMPERR

1. Where can you use the technique of SCAMMPERR?

2. How will you use it?

3. Who else could you teach SCAMMPERR to? What would be the benefit to them?

Now update your Learning Journal (page 77)

Six Thinking Hats
(Idea Generation, Selection, and Implementation)

Early in the 1980s Dr. Edward de Bono invented the Six Thinking Hats method. The method is a framework for thinking and can incorporate lateral thinking. Valuable judgmental thinking has its place in the system but is not allowed to dominate as in normal thinking.

The six hats represent six modes of thinking and are directions to think rather than labels for thinking. That is, the hats are used proactively rather than reactively.

The method promotes fuller input from more people. In de Bono's words it "separates ego from performance". Everyone is able to contribute to the exploration without denting egos as they are just using the yellow hat or whatever hat. The six hats system encourages performance rather than ego defense. People can contribute under any hat even though they initially support the opposite view.

The key point is that a hat is a direction to think rather than a label for thinking. The key theoretical reasons to use the Six Thinking Hats are to:

- encourage Parallel Thinking
- encourage full-spectrum thinking
- separate ego from performance

There are six metaphorical hats and the thinker can put on or take off one of these hats to indicate the type of thinking being used. The hats must never be used to categorize individuals, even though their behavior may seem to invite this. When done in groups, everybody wears the same hat at the same time.

Using the Six Thinking Hats

White Hat thinking

This covers facts, figures, information needs and gaps. "I think we need some white hat thinking at this point…" means: Let's drop the arguments and proposals, and look at the data base."

Questions you might ask while wearing your white hat include:

- What information do we have here?
- What information is missing?
- What information would we like to have?
- How are we going to get the information?

Red Hat thinking

This covers intuition, feelings and emotions. The red hat allows the thinker to put forward an intuition without any need to justify it. "Putting on my red hat, I think this is a terrible proposal."

Usually feelings and intuition can only be introduced into a discussion if they are supported by logic. Usually the feeling is genuine but the logic is false.

The red hat gives full permission to a thinker to put forward his or her feelings on the subject at the moment. Putting on the red hat, you express what you feel about the project.

- My gut-feeling is that this will not work.
- I don't like the way this is being done.
- This proposal is terrible.

Black Hat thinking

This is the hat of judgment and caution. It is a most valuable hat. It is not in any sense an inferior or negative hat.
The black hat is used to point out why a suggestion does not fit the facts, the available experience, the system in use, or the policy that is being followed. The black hat must always be logical.

Wearing the black hat you might consider the following:

- You can ask someone who's getting negative to take their Black Hat off for a moment - this is far more neutral than telling them to stop being so negative!
- Costs. (This proposal would be too expensive.)
- Regulations. (I don't think that the regulations would allow.)
- Design. (This design might look nice, but is not practical.)
- Tools. (These tools would mean high training costs and maintenance.)

Yellow Hat thinking

This is the logical positive. Why something will work and why it will offer benefits. It can be used in looking forward to the results of some proposed action, but can also be used to find something of value in what has already happened.

Questions you might ask when wearing the yellow hat include:

- What are the benefits of this option?
- Why is the proposal preferable?
- What are the positive assets of this design?
- How can we make it work?

Green Hat thinking

This is the hat of creativity, alternatives, proposals, what is interesting, provocations and changes. The green hat is specifically concerned with new ideas and new ways of looking at things.

This is the hat for:

- Creative thinking
- Additional alternatives
- Putting forward possibilities and hypotheses
- Interesting proposals
- New approaches

The green hat makes time and space available to focus on creative thinking. Even if no creative ideas are forthcoming, the green hat asks for the creative effort. Often green hat thinking is difficult because it goes against our habits of recognition, judgment and criticism.

Questions you might ask while wearing your green hat include:

- Are there any other ideas here?
- Are there any additional alternatives?
- Could we do this in a different way?
- Could there be another explanation?

Blue Hat thinking

The blue hat is the overview or process control. It is for organizing and controlling the thinking process so that it becomes more productive. The blue hat is for thinking about thinking. In technical terms, the blue hat is concerned with meta-cognition.

Wearing your blue hat, you might:

- Look not at the subject itself but at the "thinking" about the subject.
- Set the agenda for thinking.
- Explore the next step in the thinking, "I suggest we try some green hat thinking to get some new ideas".

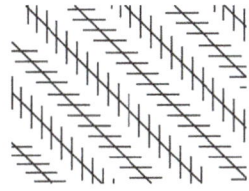

The diagonal lines are parallel!

Develop a summary, conclusion, or decision.

Complete Activity # 7
Six Thinking Hats

Complete Activity # 8
Planning your Next Meeting

ACTIVITY 7: SIX THINKING HATS

Task 1 - Practice Six Thinking Hats. Working from Home.

Imagine that your organization made a decision that all employees, regardless of position, are to work from home beginning within 30 days.

Use the Six Thinking Hats technique to work through this situation. We've given you the first hat, follow with each of the other hats in the order that they are listed. Once a hat is completed, don't go backwards. Keep focused on each hat for one minute.
(Use a timer or stopwatch if possible)

Hat	Thinking Mode	Prompting Question	Your Answer
Blue Hat	Overview / Process Control	In which sequence should we use the hats?	*Use the hats in the order listed. Only spend 1 minute on each hat.*
White	Information	What information is needed, what's available, what's missing?	
Yellow	Positive	What are the positive things about this?	
Black	Negative	What are the potential traps or pitfalls?	
Green	Creative	What ideas do you have for this situation?	

ACTIVITY 7: CONTINUED

Hat	Thinking Mode	Prompting Question	Your Answer
Red	Emotion	How do you feel about this situation at this very moment?	
Blue Hat	Overview / Process Control	In Summary, how should we proceed with this situation?	

Task 2 - Application of 6 Thinking Hats

1. Where can you use the technique of 6 Thinking Hats?

2. How will you use it?

3. Who else could you teach 6 Thinking Hats to? What would be the benefit to them?

Now update your Learning Journal (page 77)

Download the Creative Business Thinking Technique Wall Chart from https://www.catherinematttiske.com/books

© 2022, TPC - The Performance Company Pty Limited. All rights reserved.

ACTIVITY 8: PLANNING YOUR NEXT MEETING

1. When is the next team/project meeting where there will be an opportunity for you to use some of the creative business thinking techniques that you have learned in this Learning Short-take®?

Meeting Date	Team / Project Name	Start time	Finish time	Meeting Focus

2. What is the opportunity at this meeting for using creative business thinking techniques?

3. What technique/s will you use?

4. How will you use the technique/s?

5. What preparation is required prior to the meeting, in order to successfully use these techniques? (For example, preparing to teach others, using the technique on real life projects, thinking of potential outcomes, etc)

6. What materials are required?

7. How will you practice prior to the meeting to boost your confidence?

Now update your Learning Journal (page 77)

ANSWERS

ANSWERS

Mind Quiz #1

See page 10 - The Challenge

Mind-Quiz #2

It took two hours for two men to dig a hole five feet deep. How deep would it have been if 10 men had dug the hole for two hours?

The answer appears to be 25 feet deep. This answer assumes that the thinker has followed a simple mathematical relationship suggested by the description given, but we can generate *some lateral thinking ideas about what affects the size of the hole which may lead to different answers:*

- A hole may need to be of a certain size or shape so digging might stop early at a required depth.
- The deeper a hole is the more effort is required to dig it, since waste soil needs to be lifted higher to the ground level. There is a limit to how deep a hole can be dug by manpower without use of ladders or hoists for soil removal, and 25 feet is beyond this limit.
- Deeper soil layers may be harder to dig out, or we may hit rock or the water table.
- Are we digging in soil? Clay? Sand? Each presents its own special considerations.
- Holes required to be dug beyond a certain depth may require structural reinforcement to prevent collapse of the hole.
- Digging in a forest becomes much easier once we have cut through the first several feet of roots.
- Each man digging needs space to use a shovel.

- It is possible that with more people working on a project, each person may become less efficient due to increased opportunity for distraction, the assumption he become lazy, more people to talk to, etc.
- More men could work in shifts to dig faster for longer.
- There are more men but are there more shovels?
- The two hours dug by ten men may be under different weather conditions than the two hours dug by two men.
- Rain could flood the hole to prevent digging.
- Temperature conditions may freeze the men before they finish.
- Would we rather have 5 holes each 5 feet deep?
- The two men may be an engineering crew with digging machinery.
- What if one man in each group is a manager who will not actually dig?
- The extra eight men might not be strong enough to dig, or much stronger than the first two.

The most useful ideas listed above are outside the simple mathematics implied by the question.

Mind-Quiz #3

Joint Ventures

Mind-Quiz #4

A choice among alternatives

ALTERNATIVE ALTERNATIVE ALTERNATIVE
ALTERNATIVE ALTERNATIVE ALTERNATIVE
ALTERNATIVE ALTERNATIVE ALTERNATIVE
ALTERNATIVE ALTERNATIVE ALTERNATIVE
ALTERNATIVE ALTERNATIVE ALTERNATIVE
ALTERNATIVE **CHOICE** ALTERNATIVE
ALTERNATIVE ALTERNATIVE ALTERNATIVE
ALTERNATIVE ALTERNATIVE ALTERNATIVE
ALTERNATIVE ALTERNATIVE ALTERNATIVE
ALTERNATIVE ALTERNATIVE ALTERNATIVE
ALTERNATIVE ALTERNATIVE ALTERNATIVE
ALTERNATIVE ALTERNATIVE ALTERNATIVE
ALTERNATIVE ALTERNATIVE ALTERNATIVE

Mind-Quiz #5

Growing economy

Mind-Quiz #6

Work in progress

Mind-Quiz #7

Non-stop excitement

... EXCITEMENT...

Mind-Quiz #8

Divided attention

ATTEN

TION

Activity #1 - Self Assessment - Scoring & Reference

Answers to Test 1

1. party **2.** ball **3.** cheese **4.** cat **5.** club **6.** dog **7.** paper **8.** finger **9.** high **10.** sugar **11.** floor **12.** green **13.** make **14.** Dutch **15.** light

Creative individuals get 75% or more of these items correct.

The words are based upon the Remote Associates Test developed by Dr. Sarnoff A. Mednick of the University of Michigan and Dr. Sharon Halpern of the University of California, Berkeley.

Answers to Test 2

Creative individuals prefer drawings 2, 3, 5, 8 and dislike drawings 1, 4, 6, 7.

Several studies with this test have shown that creative individuals show a marked preference for the complex and asymmetrical.

These sample drawings are from the Barron-Welsh Art Scale, which consists of 86 abstract line drawings and designs which range from simple geometric forms to complex and asymmetrical figures and patterns. Several studies with this test have shown that creative individuals show a marked preference for the complex and asymmetrical. The creative individual's preference for complexity of experience is strikingly shown by this test. Several authorities feel that this test is exceedingly promising. Dr. Harrison G. Gough, an author of several effective tests, says: "If there is one single test which so far has shown promise as a forecaster of creativity, this is it."

Answers to Test 3

Highly creative individuals tend to describe themselves by these adjectives: determined, independent, inventive, enthusiastic, individualistic, industrious, absentminded, versatile, daring, dynamic, informal, impulsive, excitable, self-demanding, unassuming, worrying, thorough, sensitive, restless, reflective, preoccupied, moody.

Less creative favor adjectives such as: sincere, responsible, tolerant, clear thinking, understanding, dependable, logical, life-of-the-party, polite, popular, cheerful, obedient, polished, fashionable, stern, sociable, rational, practical, peaceable, organized, masculine, loyal, good-natured.

The adjectives are taken from the Adjective Check List, developed by Dr. Harrison G. Gough of the University of California, Berkeley. The actual test consists of 300 adjectives. Although not originally developed to assess creativity, this test has successfully differentiated highly creative individuals from less creative or non creative.

Answers to Test 4

Creative individuals tend to check these responses:
1b, 2b, 3b, 4b, 5a, 6b, 7a, 8a, 9b, 10a, 11a, 12b, 13b, 14b, 15b, 16a, 17a, 18b, 19b, 20b.

These items are based on several questionnaires used in creativity studies, including the Myers-Briggs Type Indicator, the Cree Questionnaire, California Psychological Inventory, and others.

Section 2
LEARNING JOURNAL

The Learning Journal is used throughout the process to record your key learnings, hot tips and things to remember.

Update your Learning Journal at anytime. Ensure you complete your Learning Journal after you finish each activity. Then turn back to the Learning Short-take® to continue your learning.

LEARNING JOURNAL

As you work through this Learning Short-take®, make detailed notes on this page of the lessons you have learned and any useful skill areas. For each lesson or refresher point think about how you could further develop this skill. Your coach will want to discuss these with you in your Skill Development Action Planning meeting.

"…that is what learning is.
You suddenly understand something you've understood all your life, but in a new way."

DORIS LESSING

"Act as though it were impossible to fail."

WINSTON CHURCHILL

> *"The wise do at once what the fool does later."*
> BALTASAR GRACIAN (1601-58), SPANISH JESUIT PRIEST AND AUTHOR.

Learning or Idea	Action to be taken	Result Expected

Learning Journal - continued

Learning or Idea	Action to be taken	Result Expected

> *"Anyone who stops learning is old, whether at twenty or eighty."*
> HENRY FORD

Learning or Idea	Action to be taken	Result Expected

"

*"Imagination grows by exercise,
and contrary to common belief,
is more powerful in the mature than
in the young."*

W. SOMERSET MAUGHAM

Section 3

SKILL DEVELOPMENT ACTION PLAN

Your Skill Development Action Plan is the last Step in the process. After you have completed the Learning Short-take® and all Activities, update your Learning Journal, then complete this section.

SKILL DEVELOPMENT ACTION PLAN

This is the most important part of the program - your individual Skill Development Action Plan.

You need to complete this plan before meeting with your manager or prior to on-going coaching. You will discuss it in detail with your manager or coach as he or she will ensure that you have everything you need to complete the tasks and activities.

Once you have completed your **Skill Development Action Plan** schedule a meeting time with your manager or coach to review your plan. Take your Learning Short-take® and all other documentation received during the training course to this meeting.

Remember - you have committed to your **Skill Development Action Plan**, and need to make time to complete your tasks!

> *"The mind, once stretched by a new idea, never regains its original dimensions."*
>
> OLIVER WENDELL HOLMES

> *"Whatever you can do or dream you can - begin it. Boldness has genius, power and magic."*
>
> JOHANN WOLFGANG VON GOETHE

"Imagination is the eye of the soul."
JOSEPH JOUBERT (1754-1824)

Task or activity (Be specific)	Measure (this will help you to know you have achieved it)	Date (Be specific)
Reflect on your Learning Journal. Transfer action items that you can apply to your job. Ensure that you include some 'stretch goals' and also a blend of short, medium and long term goals.	Apart from you, who else is needed to assist you in achieving your goal.	Be specific. A general date such as 'Quarter 1', 'August', or 'by end of year' is vague and more likely to result in not achieving your target. Be specific – e.g. 22nd November.

IDEAS FOR DISCUSSION WITH MY MANAGER

Ideas

CONGRATULATIONS!

You've now completed this Learning Short-take®.

Meet with your Manager/Coach to discuss your
Skill Development Action Plan.

"

"Imagination is more important than knowledge. For while knowledge defines all we currently know and understand, imagination points to all we might yet discover and create."

ALBERT EINSTEIN

QUICK REFERENCE

This Quick Reference provides you with a summary of key concepts, models and reference material from Learning Short-takes®. We have also included some quotations to ponder.

Use this section as a quick reference to keep your learning active.

Quick Reference

Creativity Defined

Creativity is bringing an item, a method or an idea, which did not previously exist, into reality.

What is Creative Thinking?

Creative thinking is the process in which we construct a new idea. It is the merging of ideas that have not been put together before.

Quick Reference

> **Anyone can be creative provided they learn and develop their skills.**

Edward DeBono

Lateral Thinking

Lateral Thinking™ is a more *systematic* approach to creativity by deliberately using specific steps and techniques to think creatively. Instead of relying solely on logic, lateral thinking is a deliberate, systematic process to think differently.

Quick Reference

3 Limiting Beliefs

The primary blocks to our creative potential seem to originate from the limiting beliefs of a left-brain world:

- I am not creative
- It's not okay to be creative round here
- I don't know how to be creative

> **The answer to your problem 'pre-exists'. You need to ask the right question to reveal the answer.**

Charles Chic Thompson

Quick Reference

Enhancing Personal Creativity

1. Create a creative atmosphere
2. Focus on a situation or goal
3. Maintain determination
4. Don't get it right, get it written

> **No problem is insurmountable. With a little courage, teamwork and determination a person can overcome anything.**

B. Dodge

Quick Reference

1. Alternative Scenarios
(Situation definition, Idea Implementation)

Scenarios are developed specifically for a particular problem. To begin developing scenarios:

- State the specific decision that needs to be made.
- Identify the major forces that impact the decision.
- Build four scenarios based on each of the major forces.
- Examine the links and synergies of opportunities across the range of scenarios.

2. Brainstorming
(Idea Generation)

- Use a large whiteboard or flipchart paper.
- Write question or issue on board/paper.
- Appoint a person as a scribe.
- Ideal group size 7-10. No more than 15.
- Have the group define the outcome of the session.
- Ask for crazy ideas early in the brainstorming session.
- Ensure no criticism.
- Seek a large number of ideas.
- Link different ideas together.
- Keep the pace fast.
- Be aware of group energy.
- If the group is stuck
  - use the 'unlimited budget' scenario.

Quick Reference

3. BrainWriting
(Idea Generation)

BrainWriting is a technique similar to Brainstorming. The general process is that all ideas are recorded by the individual who thought of them. They are then passed on to the next person who uses them as a trigger for their own ideas.

- BrainWriting Pool
- Constrained BrainWriting
- BrainWriting 6-3-5.

4. Do Nothing
(Idea Generation)

We often make the assumption that something must be done about a particular issue/problem, but what happens if we "do nothing"?

Stop and think for a while, either alone or as a group, about the outcomes if nothing was done.

5. DO IT
(Situation Definition & Idea Selection)

D - **D**efine problem or situation

O - **O**pen mind and apply creative techniques

I - **I**dentify best solution

T - **T**ransform

6. Metaphors
(Situation Definition, Idea Generation)

- Call attention to metaphors when they are expressed and reflect on the implications, such as what they suggest about assumptions people are holding.

- Invite people to brainstorm metaphors for a particular situation with which a group is struggling.

- Use metaphors that speak from broad experiences common to the group, helping people become connected to the situation.

Quick Reference

7. Mind Mapping
(Situation Definition or Idea Generation)

Basic Mind Mapping Steps

- Start in the center with an image of the topic, using at least 3 colors.
- Use images, symbols, codes and dimensions throughout your mindmap.
- Each key word/image must be alone and sitting on its own line.
- The lines must be connected, starting from the central image. The central lines are thicker, organic and flowing, becoming thinner as they radiate out from the center.
- Make the lines the same length as the word/image.
- Use colors - make up your own code - throughout the mind map.
- Develop your own personal style of mind mapping.

8. Random Input
(Idea Generation)

Randomly pick up a magazine and read one article, no matter how remote its subject is to your challenge.

Then contemplate the connections between the article and your challenge; try to generate some new ideas.

Any such exercise is extremely valuable in helping you set up and cultivate habits that encourage random input.

Quick Reference

9. RoleStorming
(Idea Generation)

RoleStorming is an evolution of Brainstorming, whereby you take on another identity. Viewing problems and solutions from a different standpoint.

10. SCAMMPERR
(Idea Generation)

S - Substitute - components, materials, people

C - Combine - mix, combine with other assemblies or services, integrate

A - Adapt - alter, change function, use part of another element

M - Magnify - make it enormous, longer, higher, overstated, added features

M - Modify - increase or reduce in scale, change shape, modify attributes (e.g. color)

P - Put to another use

E - Eliminate - remove elements, simplify, reduce to core functionality

R - Rearrange - change the order, interchange components, change the speed or other pattern.

R - Reverse - turn inside out or upside down.

Quick Reference

11. Six Thinking Hats
(Idea Generation, Selection, and Implementation)

Information
facts, data

Emotion
how do you feel about this?

Judgment
caution, risks, logical negative

Positive
benefits

Creative
growth, ideas, alternatives

Overview & Process control
agenda, summary

> **Creativity is inventing, experimenting, growing, taking risks, breaking rules, making mistakes, and having fun.**
>
> Mary Lou Cook

"

"It is better to have enough ideas for some of them to be wrong, than to be always right by having no ideas at all."

EDWARD DE BONO

NEXT STEPS

Congratulations! You have now completed this Learning Short-take® title. The entire list of Learning Short-takes® can be found on the catherinemattiske.com website.

In this section we have suggested Learning Short-take® titles for you that will build your learning. You may order these Learning Short-takes® online at https://www.catherinemattiske.com/books or from your bookstores.

Confident Facilitation Skills
Tools and Techniques for the Professional Facilitator

Learning Short-take® Outline

Confident Facilitation Skills combines self-study with realistic workplace activities to provide you with the key skills and techniques to become a more effective facilitator. You will be guided through a comprehensive approach to prepare for a facilitation session, focus the group, draw out ideas, manage difficult behavior, build consensus, maintain high energy, close the session, and construct customized agendas. **Confident Facilitation Skills** also includes a comprehensive reference guide of proven group facilitation techniques.

Facilitation is fast becoming a key skill for anyone who is in a team, leading a project team, heading up a working group, or managing a department. Facilitation is the skill and art of guiding others to solve problems to achieve objectives without personally giving advice or offering solutions. A facilitator provides the structure and process - enabling groups to function effectively and make high-quality decisions.

Confident Facilitation Skills includes the **Confident Facilitation Initial Meeting Tool**, provided to you as a free download.

Learning Objectives
- Define the role of a facilitator.
- Identify the key facilitation principles.
- Describe best practices related to each facilitation principle.
- Be able to differentiate between process and content facilitation.
- Identify the core practices and skills required for effective facilitation.
- Explain how to stimulate group participation and positively handle conflict.
- Create a Skill Development Action Plan.

Course Content
- Part 1: Facilitation Defined
- Part 2: The Role of the Facilitator
- Part 3: Key Principles of Facilitation
- Part 4: Content versus Process
- Part 5: Encouraging Group Participation
- Part 6: Managing Group Conflict

www.catherinemattiske.com

www.ingramcontent.com/pod-product-compliance
Lightning Source LLC
Chambersburg PA
CBHW042230090526
44587CB00001B/11